WORDS
OF THE
Savior

WORDS
OF THE
Savior

DESERET
BOOK

SALT LAKE CITY, UTAH

Compilation © 2014 Deseret Book Company

All rights reserved. No part of this book may be reproduced in any form or by any means without permission in writing from the publisher, Deseret Book Company, at permissions@deseretbook.com or P. O. Box 30178, Salt Lake City, Utah 84130. This work is not an official publication of The Church of Jesus Christ of Latter-day Saints. The views expressed herein are the responsibility of the author and do not necessarily represent the position of the Church or of Deseret Book Company.

DESERET BOOK is a registered trademark of Deseret Book Company.

Visit us at DeseretBook.com

Library of Congress Cataloging-in-Publication Data
(CIP data on file)
ISBN 978-1-60907-993-2

Printed in China
Four Colour Print Group
10   9   8   7   6   5   4   3   2   1

*A*sk, and it shall be given you; seek, and ye shall find; knock, and it shall be opened unto you: For every one that asketh receiveth; and he that seeketh findeth; and to him that knocketh it shall be opened.

MATTHEW 7:7–8

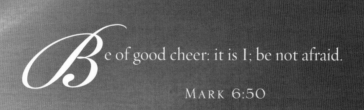

$\mathcal{B}$e of good cheer: it is I; be not afraid.

MARK 6:50

Ye are the salt of the earth: but if the salt have lost his savour, wherewith shall it be salted? it is thenceforth good for nothing, but to be cast out, and to be trodden under foot of men.

MATTHEW 5:13

Ye call me Master and Lord: and ye say well; for so I am. If I then, your Lord and Master, have washed your feet; ye also ought to wash one another's feet. For I have given you an example, that ye should do as I have done to you. Verily, verily, I say unto you, The servant is not greater than his lord; neither he that is sent greater than he that sent him. If ye know these things, happy are ye if ye do them.

JOHN 13:13–17

I CAN OF MINE OWN SELF

DO NOTHING: AS I HEAR,

I JUDGE: AND MY JUDGMENT

IS JUST; BECAUSE I SEEK NOT

MINE OWN WILL, BUT THE

WILL OF THE *Father*

WHICH HATH SENT ME.

JOHN 5:30

*S*trive to enter in at the strait gate: for many, I say unto you, will seek to enter in, and shall not be able.

LUKE 13:24

*T*ake heed to yourselves: If thy brother trespass against thee, rebuke him; and if he repent, forgive him. And if he trespass against thee seven times in a day, and seven times in a day turn again to thee, saying, I repent; thou shalt forgive him.

LUKE 17:3–4

*B*lessed are the poor in spirit: for theirs is the kingdom of heaven. Blessed are they that mourn: for they shall be comforted. Blessed are the meek: for they shall inherit the earth. Blessed are they which do hunger and thirst after righteousness: for they shall be filled. Blessed are the merciful: for they shall obtain mercy. Blessed are the pure in heart: for they shall see God. Blessed are the peacemakers: for they shall be called the children of God. Blessed are they which are persecuted for righteousness' sake: for theirs is the kingdom of heaven. Blessed are ye, when men shall revile you, and persecute you, and shall say all manner of evil against you falsely, for my sake. Rejoice, and be exceeding glad: for great is your reward in heaven.

MATTHEW 5:3–12

Verily I say unto you, Except ye be converted, and become as little children, ye shall not enter into the kingdom of heaven. Whosoever therefore shall humble himself as this little child, the same is greatest in the kingdom of heaven. And whoso shall receive one such little child in my name receiveth me. . . . For where two or three are gathered together in my name, there am I in the midst of them.

MATTHEW 18:3–5, 20

I am the bread of life: he that cometh to me shall never hunger; and he that believeth on me shall never thirst.

JOHN 6:35

If thou canst believe,

all things

are possible

TO HIM THAT BELIEVETH.

MARK 9:23

I say unto you, If ye have faith as a grain of mustard seed, ye shall say unto this mountain, Remove hence to yonder place; and it shall remove; and nothing shall be impossible unto you.

MATTHEW 17:20

*T*hey that are whole have no need of the physician, but they that are sick: I came not to call the righteous, but sinners to repentance.

MARK 2:17

*W*hy are ye so fearful? how is it that ye have no faith?

MARK 4:40

Peace, be still

*L*ay not up for yourselves treasures upon earth, where moth and rust doth corrupt, and where thieves break through and steal: but lay up for yourselves treasures in heaven, where neither moth nor rust doth corrupt, and where thieves do not break through nor steal: for where your treasure is, there will your heart be also.

MATTHEW 6:19–21

Yea rather,
blessed
ARE THEY THAT HEAR
THE WORD OF GOD,
AND *keep it.*

LUKE 11:28

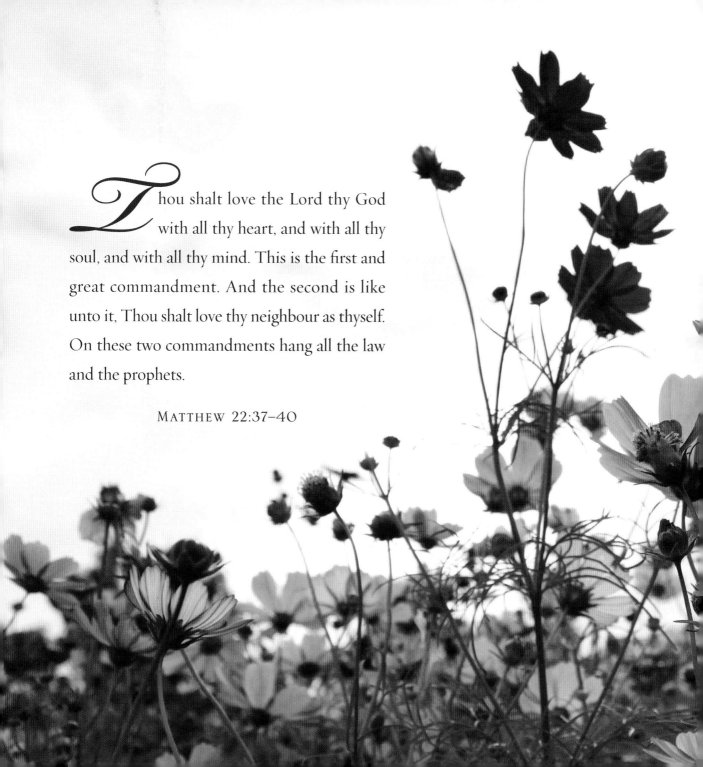

Thou shalt love the Lord thy God with all thy heart, and with all thy soul, and with all thy mind. This is the first and great commandment. And the second is like unto it, Thou shalt love thy neighbour as thyself. On these two commandments hang all the law and the prophets.

MATTHEW 22:37–40

After this manner therefore pray ye: Our Father which art in heaven, Hallowed be thy name. Thy kingdom come. Thy will be done in earth, as it is in heaven. Give us this day our daily bread. And forgive us our debts, as we forgive our debtors. And lead us not into temptation, but deliver us from evil: For thine is the kingdom, and the power, and the glory, for ever. Amen.

*W*hile ye have light, believe in the light, that ye may be the children of light.

JOHN 12:36

*H*e that believeth on me, believeth not on me, but on him that sent me. And he that seeth me seeth him that sent me. I am come a light into the world, that whosoever believeth on me should not abide in darkness. And if any man hear my words, and believe not, I judge him not: for I came not to judge the world, but to save the world.

JOHN 12:44–47

Consider the lilies how they grow: they toil not, they spin not; and yet I say unto you, that Solomon in all his glory was not arrayed like one of these. If then God so clothe the grass, which is to day in the field, and to morrow is cast into the oven; how much more will he clothe you, O ye of little faith? And seek not ye what ye shall eat, or what ye shall drink, neither be ye of doubtful mind. For all these things do the nations of the world seek after: and your Father knoweth that ye have need of these things. But rather seek ye the kingdom of God; and all these things shall be added unto you.

LUKE 12:27–31

*H*e that is without sin among you,
let him first cast a stone at her.

JOHN 8:7

*R*ender therefore unto Cæsar
the things which are Cæsar's;
and unto God the things that are God's.

Matthew 22:21

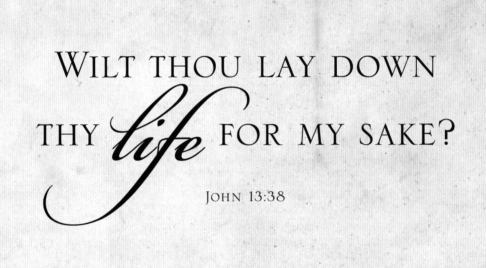

WILT THOU LAY DOWN
THY *life* FOR MY SAKE?

JOHN 13:38

*C*ome ye after me, and I will make you to become fishers of men.

Mark 1:17

*A*rise, and be not afraid.

MATTHEW 17:7

*B*lessed art thou, Simon Bar-jona: for flesh and blood hath not revealed it unto thee, but my Father which is in heaven. And I say also unto thee, That thou art Peter, and upon this rock I will build my church; and the gates of hell shall not prevail against it. And I will give unto thee the keys of the kingdom of heaven: and whatsoever thou shalt bind on earth shall be bound in heaven: and whatsoever thou shalt loose on earth shall be loosed in heaven.

MATTHEW 16:17–19

*I*f any man will come after me, let him deny himself, and take up his cross, and follow me. For whosoever will save his life shall lose it: and whosoever will lose his life for my sake shall find it. For what is a man profited, if he shall gain the whole world, and lose his own soul? or what shall a man give in exchange for his soul? For the Son of man shall come in the glory of his Father with his angels; and then he shall reward every man according to his works.

MATTHEW 16:24–27

*J*udge not, that ye be not judged. For with what judgment ye judge, ye shall be judged: and with what measure ye mete, it shall be measured to you again. And why beholdest thou the mote that is in thy brother's eye, but considerest not the beam that is in thine own eye? Or how wilt thou say to thy brother, Let me pull out the mote out of thine eye; and, behold, a beam is in thine own eye? Thou hypocrite, first cast out the beam out of thine own eye; and then shalt thou see clearly to cast out the mote out of thy brother's eye.

MATTHEW 7:1–5

*A*re not five sparrows sold for two farthings, and not one of them is forgotten before God? But even the very hairs of your head are all numbered. Fear not therefore: ye are of more value than many sparrows.

Luke 12:6–7

AND ALL THINGS,
WHATSOEVER YE
SHALL ASK IN
prayer,
BELIEVING,
YE SHALL RECEIVE.

MATTHEW 21:22

Verily I say unto you, that this generation shall not pass, till all these things be done. Heaven and earth shall pass away: but my words shall not pass away. But of that day and that hour knoweth no man, no, not the angels which are in heaven, neither the Son, but the Father. Take ye heed, watch and pray: for ye know not when the time is.

MARK 13:30–33

*B*ehold, a sower went forth to sow; and when he sowed, some seeds fell by the way side, and the fowls came and devoured them up: some fell upon stony places, where they had not much earth: and forthwith they sprung up, because they had no deepness of earth: and when the sun was up, they were scorched; and because they had no root, they withered away. And some fell among thorns; and the thorns sprung up, and choked them: but other fell into good ground, and brought forth fruit, some an hundredfold, some sixtyfold, some thirtyfold. Who hath ears to hear, let him hear.

MATTHEW 13:3–9

*T*hen shall the kingdom of heaven be likened unto ten virgins, which took their lamps, and went forth to meet the bridegroom. And five of them were wise, and five were foolish. They that were foolish took their lamps, and took no oil with them: but the wise took oil in their vessels with their lamps. . . . And at midnight there was a cry made, Behold, the bridegroom cometh; go ye out to meet him. Then all those virgins arose, and trimmed their lamps. And the foolish said unto the wise, Give us of your oil; for our lamps are gone out. But the wise answered, saying, Not so; lest there be not enough for us and you: but go ye rather to them that sell, and buy for yourselves. And while they went to buy, the bridegroom came; and they that were ready went in with him to the marriage: and the door was shut. . . . Watch therefore, for ye know neither the day nor the hour wherein the Son of man cometh.

MATTHEW 25:1–4, 6–10, 13

$\mathcal{C}$ome unto me, all ye that labour and are heavy laden, and I will give you rest. Take my yoke upon you, and learn of me; for I am meek and lowly in heart: and ye shall find rest unto your souls. For my yoke is easy, and my burden is light.

MATTHEW 11:28–30

RISE UP, AND

stand forth

IN THE MIDST.

LUKE 6:8

Verily, verily, I say unto thee, Except a man be born again, he cannot see the kingdom of God. . . . Verily, verily, I say unto thee, Except a man be born of water and of the Spirit, he cannot enter into the kingdom of God.

JOHN 3:3, 5

O Jerusalem, Jerusalem, which killest the prophets, and stonest them that are sent unto thee; how often would I have gathered thy children together, as a hen doth gather her brood under her wings, and ye would not!

Behold, your house is left unto you desolate: and verily I say

unto you, Ye shall not see me, until the time come when ye shall

say, Blessed is he that cometh in the name of the Lord.

LUKE 13:34–35

Whosoever shall receive this child in my name receiveth me: and whosoever shall receive me receiveth him that sent me: for he that is least among you all, the same shall be great.

LUKE 9:48

*S*eest thou this woman? I entered into thine house, thou gavest me no water for my feet: but she hath washed my feet with tears, and wiped them with the hairs of her head. Thou gavest me no kiss: but this woman since the time I came in hath not ceased to kiss my feet. My head with oil thou didst not anoint: but this woman hath anointed my feet with ointment. Wherefore I say unto thee, Her sins, which are many, are forgiven; for she loved much: but to whom little is forgiven, the same loveth little.

Luke 7:44–47

From the beginning of the creation God made them male and female. For this cause shall a man leave his father and mother, and cleave to his wife; and they twain shall be one flesh: so then they are no more twain, but one flesh. What therefore God hath joined together, let not man put asunder.

MARK 10:6–9

*I*t is not for you to know the times or the seasons, which the Father hath put in his own power. But ye shall receive power, after that the Holy Ghost is come upon you: and ye shall be witnesses unto me both in Jerusalem, and in all Judæa, and in Samaria, and unto the uttermost part of the earth.

ACTS 1:7–8

GO YE THEREFORE, AND
teach all nations,
BAPTIZING THEM IN THE NAME
OF THE FATHER, AND OF THE
SON, AND OF THE HOLY GHOST:
TEACHING THEM TO OBSERVE
ALL THINGS WHATSOEVER I HAVE
COMMANDED YOU: AND, LO, I AM
WITH YOU ALWAY, EVEN UNTO
THE END OF THE WORLD.

MATTHEW 28:19–20

The Son can do nothing of himself, but what he seeth the Father do: for what things soever he doeth, these also doeth the Son likewise. For the Father loveth the Son, and sheweth him all things that himself doeth: and he will shew him greater works than these, that ye may marvel. For as the Father raiseth up the dead, and quickeneth them; even so the Son quickeneth whom he will. For the Father judgeth no man, but hath committed all judgment unto the Son: that all men should honour the Son, even as they honour the Father.

JOHN 5:19–23

*W*ith men this is impossible; but with God all things are possible.

MATTHEW 19:26

Come and follow me

WHERE IS YOUR *faith?*

LUKE 8:25

Therefore whosoever heareth these sayings of mine, and doeth them, I will liken him unto a wise man, which built his house upon a rock: And the rain descended, and the floods came, and the winds blew, and beat upon that house; and it fell not: for it was founded upon a rock. And every one that heareth these sayings of mine, and doeth them not, shall be likened unto a foolish man, which built his house upon the sand: And the rain descended, and the floods came, and the winds blew, and beat upon that house; and it fell: and great was the fall of it.

MATTHEW 7:24–27

*I*f ye continue in my word, then are ye my disciples indeed; and ye shall know the truth, and the truth shall make you free.

JOHN 8:31–32

Ye are my disciples

My *doctrine*

IS NOT MINE,

BUT HIS THAT

SENT ME.

JOHN 7:16

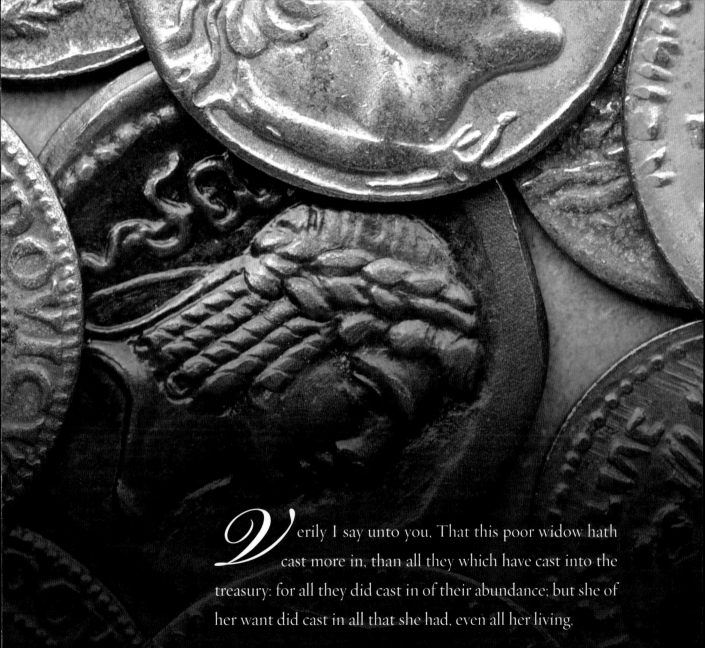

*V*erily I say unto you, That this poor widow hath cast more in, than all they which have cast into the treasury: for all they did cast in of their abundance; but she of her want did cast in all that she had, even all her living.

*S*omebody hath touched me: for I perceive that
virtue is gone out of me. . . . Be of good comfort:
thy faith hath made thee whole; go in peace.

LUKE 8:46, 48

WHAT WOULD YE
THAT I SHOULD
DO FOR *you?*

MARK 10:36

*A*ccording to your faith be it unto you.

MATTHEW 9:29

*W*hat man of you, having an hundred sheep, if he lose one of them, doth not leave the ninety and nine in the wilderness, and go after that which is lost, until he find it? And when he hath found it, he layeth it on his shoulders, rejoicing. And when he cometh home, he calleth together his friends and neighbours, saying unto them, Rejoice with me; for I have found my sheep which was lost. I say unto you, that likewise joy shall be in heaven over one sinner that repenteth, more than over ninety and nine just persons, which need no repentance.

LUKE 15:4–7

*S*uffer the little children to come unto me, and forbid them not: for of such is the kingdom of God. Verily I say unto you, Whosoever shall not receive the kingdom of God as a little child, he shall not enter therein.

MARK 10:14–15

Ye know not what ye ask: can ye drink of the cup that I drink of? and be baptized with the baptism that I am baptized with? . . .

Ye shall indeed drink of the cup that I drink of; and with the baptism that I am baptized withal shall ye be baptized:

But to sit on my right hand and on my left hand is not mine to give; but it shall be given to them for whom it is prepared.

MARK 10:38–40

Take heed that no man deceive you. For many shall come in my name, saying, I am Christ; and shall deceive many. And ye shall hear of wars and rumours of wars: see that ye be not troubled: for all these things must come to pass, but the end is not yet. For nation shall rise against nation, and kingdom against kingdom: and there shall be famines, and pestilences, and earthquakes, in divers places. All these are the beginning of sorrows.

MATTHEW 24:4–8

Ye have not chosen me, but I have chosen you, and ordained you, that ye should go and bring forth fruit, and that your fruit should remain: that whatsoever ye shall ask of the Father in my name, he may give it you.

JOHN 15:16

YE ARE THE

light

OF THE WORLD.

MATTHEW 5:14

*B*lessed are the eyes which see the things that ye see: for I tell you, that many prophets and kings have desired to see those things which ye see, and have not seen them; and to hear those things which ye hear, and have not heard them.

LUKE 10:23–24

For God so loved
the world, that he gave
his only begotten Son,
that whosoever
believeth in him should
not perish, but have
everlasting life.

John 3:16

I am the good shepherd: the good shepherd giveth his life for the sheep.

JOHN 10:11

Behold, we go up to Jerusalem; and the Son of man shall be betrayed unto the chief priests and unto the scribes, and they shall condemn him to death, and shall deliver him to the Gentiles to mock, and to scourge, and to crucify him: and the third day he shall rise again.

MATTHEW 20:18–19

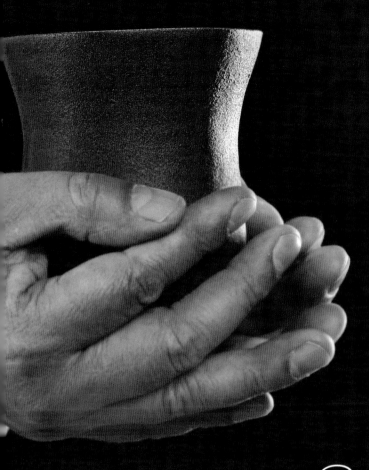

*T*his is my body which is given for you: this do in remembrance of me. Likewise also the cup after supper, saying, This cup is the new testament in my blood, which is shed for you.

LUKE 22:19–20

*L*et not your heart be troubled: ye believe in God, believe also in me.

In my Father's house are many mansions: if it were not so, I would have told you. I go to prepare a place for you.

And if I go and prepare a place for you, I will come again, and receive you unto myself; that where I am, there ye may be also.

And whither I go ye know, and the way ye know.

JOHN 14:1–4

I am the way, the truth, and the life: no man cometh unto the Father, but by me.

JOHN 14:6

O my Father, if it be possible, let this cup pass from me; nevertheless not as I will, but as thou wilt.

MATTHEW 26:39

Not my will, but thine

*F*ather, forgive them; for they know not what they do.

LUKE 23:34

Therefore be ye also ready: for in such an hour as ye think not the Son of man cometh. . . . Blessed is that servant, whom his lord when he cometh shall find so doing. Verily I say unto you, That he shall make him ruler over all his goods.

MATTHEW 24:44, 46–47

HEREAFTER SHALL YE SEE THE

Son of man

SITTING ON THE RIGHT HAND OF POWER, AND COMING IN THE CLOUDS OF HEAVEN.

MATTHEW 26:64

*W*hy are ye troubled? and why do thoughts arise in your hearts? Behold my hands and my feet, that it is I myself: handle me, and see; for a spirit hath not flesh and bones, as ye see me have.

Luke 24:38–39

GOD IS NOT THE
GOD OF THE DEAD,
BUT OF THE *living.*

MATTHEW 22:32

*V*erily, verily, I say unto you, The hour is coming, and now is, when the dead shall hear the voice of the Son of God: and they that hear shall live. For as the Father hath life in himself; so hath he given to the Son to have life in himself.

JOHN 5:25–26

I am Alpha and Omega, the beginning and the ending. . . . Fear not; I am the first and the last: I am he that liveth, and was dead; and, behold, I am alive for evermore, Amen; and have the keys of hell and of death.

REVELATION 1:8, 17–18

This is my commandment, That ye love one another, as I have loved you. Greater love hath no man than this, that a man lay down his life for his friends.

JOHN 15:12–13

Photo Credits